# A walk from

# Our Village School

## Deborah Chancellor • Chris Fairclough

**W**

# FRANKLIN WATTS
LONDON • SYDNEY

*First published in 2014*
*by Franklin Watts*

*Copyright © Franklin Watts 2014*

*Franklin Watts*
*338 Euston Road*
*London NW1 3BH*

*Franklin Watts Australia*
*Level 17/207 Kent Street*
*Sydney, NSW 2000*

*Series editor: Sarah Peutrill*
*Series designer: Jane Hawkins*
*Photographer: Chris Fairclough*
*Illustrations: John Alston*

*Every attempt has been made to clear copyright. Should there be any inadvertent*
*omission please apply to the publisher for rectification.*

*With thanks to the staff and children at the Great Chesterford C of E Primary*
*Academy, Great Chesterford, Essex.*

*Dewey number: 910.9'1734*

*HB ISBN:  978 1 4451 2748 4*
*Library ebook ISBN: 978 1 4451 2752 1*

*Printed in China*

*Franklin Watts is a division of Hachette Children's Books,*
*an Hachette UK company.*
*www.hachette.co.uk*

# Contents

Words in **bold** are in the glossary on page 29.

# Country walk

Alex, Jaan, Jodie and Leah want to go for a walk near their school. They live in a small village called Great Chesterford, which is in the **county** of Essex, in the south east of the **UK**. The children's school is called Great Chesterford Church of England Academy.

The children use different kinds of map to plan their **route**. They look at **large scale maps** of the local area.

They also go online to find a satellite map, which is made up of images taken from a space satellite.

The children think carefully about their walk. They want to plan a route that will start at the school, take them all around the village, and help them to answer some questions about the place where they live.

1. Are there any religious buildings?

2. How busy are the village roads?

3. Are there many places of work?

4. How old are some of the houses?

5. What sports can you play?

*Some parts of the school are brand new (above), and others date back to **Victorian** times (left).*

## Focus on History

The village sign shows an old **steam train** at Great Chesterford Station. In the past, steam trains used to stop near the village. Today, you can catch fast electric trains at the village station. These trains go to London and Cambridge.

GREAT CHESTERFORD

# Setting off

The children and their teacher get ready to go on the walk. They need to take a map and a **compass**, to help them find their way. They also want some clipboards, paper and pencils for writing or drawing and a camera for taking photos.

The teacher downloads a **pedometer app** onto her **smartphone**, so the group can measure how far they walk. The distance is shown in kilometres, and the time the walk takes is shown in hours, minutes and seconds.

*The **GPS** on the teacher's phone helps the children follow the route.*

# SCHOOL STREET

**How old is the oldest building near you?**

Alex, Jaan, Jodie and Leah leave the school and turn left into a road called School Street. They walk south down this road. They stop to look at some of the houses. There is a date on the wall of one house, which helps the children work out how old the building is.

*The village school was built in 1849.*

## Focus on History

The date on this house reads 1841. This was soon after Queen Victoria came to the throne, over 170 years ago.

# Local church

Alex, Jaan, Jodie and Leah walk down School Street until they come to a road called Church Street. Both these road names give clues about things to find in the village. The children turn right into Church Street and head for the church.

**CHURCH STREET**

Q: Are there any religious buildings?

A: There is a very old church in the village.

*Some pavements in the village are very narrow.*

*The church is the tallest and oldest building in the village.*

The children go through a gate into the **churchyard**. Their teacher tells them different parts of the church were built at different times in the past.

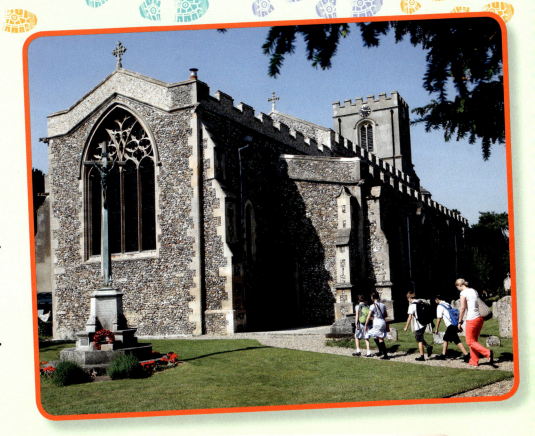

*Focus on History*
There has been a church in Great Chesterford for eight **centuries**. Some parts of the building were built about 800 years ago, when King John I ruled England.

The group leaves the churchyard, turns right and goes back down Church Street. They keep walking until the name of the road changes to South Street. This road is to the south of the village. The children check the GPS on their teacher's phone, to see exactly where they are now.

# By the river

Alex, Jaan, Jodie and Leah come to the village green, which is next to a river. As they walk over to the riverbank, they pass a red telephone box. Their teacher explains that people can use the **public pay phone** inside to make phone calls. However, most people use mobile phones.

*The river by the village green is called the River Cam. This river also flows through the city of Cambridge, about 20 kilometres north of Great Chesterford.*

**?** Is there a river near where you live? What is it called?

*Rivers and other natural features are shown on maps. Can you find this river on the map opposite?*

The children stop to look at the river plants and wildlife. They spot some water lilies, a few ducks and a couple of dragonflies.

The children look across the river at the fields and countryside. There is lots of open space. They are on the south side of the village and there are not many houses or roads to see in this direction.

**FOCUS ON SCIENCE**
The water in the River Cam is clear and **unpolluted**, so it is full of life. Many different kinds of fish swim in this river, for example sticklebacks and trout.

# Village pub

Alex, Jaan, Jodie and Leah have a quick rest and a drink by the riverbank. Then they leave the village green and walk back to South Street. They turn right and walk towards a **crossroads**. The children look carefully before they cross the road.

There is hardly any traffic in the village, but *pedestrians* must still watch out for cars.

**?** Is there much traffic near your school?

Q: How busy are the village roads?

A: The roads in the village are quiet. There are no traffic lights or roundabouts.

# HIGH STREET

On the other side of the crossroads, the road name changes again. It is no longer 'South Street', but is now the 'High Street'. On the right there is a pub called 'The Crown and Thistle.'

*The village pub is a popular local meeting place.*

The children stop outside the pub to check the map. They spot a date on the wall of the pub – it says 1825. Parts of the building are actually about 500 years old and date back to Tudor times. The pub was built in 1528 and has had different names since then.

*Large scale maps use symbols to show local landmarks and public buildings.*

# Local farm

The pub is on the corner of the High Street and Manor Lane. Alex, Jaan, Jodie and Leah walk down Manor Lane towards a farm called Manor Farm. They see two big **storehouses**. One of them is new, and the other is about a hundred years old. Both buildings are used to store farm machinery.

? Do you live near a farm?

The group follow a footpath out into the countryside.

*Rape seed is growing in the fields. This **crop** will be used for animal feed and to make vegetable oil.*

PUBLIC FOOTPATH

Jaan takes some photos of the plants he can see. Most of them are part of the crop, but some are wild flowers.

*Wild flowers*

*Rape seed pods*

The footpath takes the children back into the village. They walk up Rose Lane, which leads to the High Street. The group stops in Rose Lane to look at the cottages. They notice that most of the roofs have tiles, but one of them has a **thatched roof**.

**FOCUS ON SCIENCE**
The roof of this thatched cottage is made of dried reeds. This keeps the house warm in winter and cool in summer.

# High Street

The High Street is the main road that passes through the village. Alex, Jaan, Jodie and Leah turn right out of Rose Lane and walk a short distance up the High Street.

**ROSE LANE**
**NOT SUITABLE FOR HGV'S**

*Big trucks (HGVs) cannot drive along the narrow village roads.*

The children stop for 15 minutes to see how many **vehicles** drive past them on the High Street. They count the bikes, motorbikes, cars and buses that pass by. It is very quiet on the village High Street. The children only see two bikes and six cars.

HIGH STREET

**FOCUS ON GEOGRAPHY**
This is a busy **doctors' surgery**. People come here from Great Chesterford and other nearby villages. Most small villages do not have their own doctors' surgery.

The children would like to go shopping but there are no shops on the High Street, just houses and a doctors' surgery. There are not many **local businesses** in Great Chesterford, so most people travel away from the village to shop or to go to work.

Q: Are there many places of work?

A: There are not many shops or offices in the village.

# Work and play

Alex, Jodie, Jaan and Leah cross back over the High Street. They pass a bus stop. Not many buses drive through the village, so most people use a car, a bike or take the train.

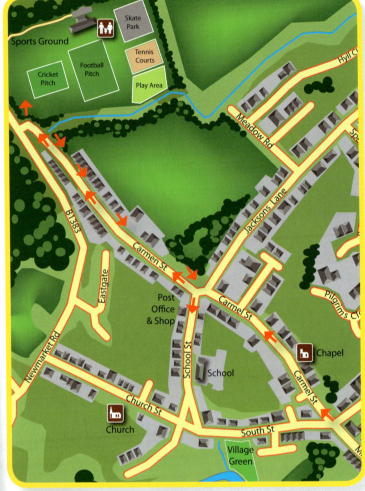

The children walk up Carmel Street. They cross Jacksons Lane to Carmen Street. The village **sports ground** is at the end of this road. It has a cricket and a football pitch, a skate park and a tennis court. The children run over to the playground.

Q: What sports can you play?

A: You can play football, cricket or tennis at the sports ground. You can also take your skateboard or BMX bike to the skate park.

The children leave the sports ground and walk back the way they came. At a crossroads, they turn right into School Street. The village shop is just ahead of them.

| Shop Opening Times | |
|---|---|
| Monday | 6.30am - 7.30pm |
| Tuesday | 6.30am - 7.30pm |
| Wednesday | 6.30am - 7.30pm |
| Thursday | 6.30am - 7.30pm |
| Friday | 6.30am - 7.30pm |
| Saturday | 7.30am - 6.00pm |
| Sunday | 8.00am - 12.00pm |

This is the only shop in Great Chesterford. From Monday to Friday, it is open from 6.30am to 7.30pm. At weekends, the opening hours are shorter.

? Do the shops open late near you?

*The village shop closes early on Sunday.*

# Back to school

The children leave the shop and walk along School Street. Leah and Jodie check their direction on a compass. They are heading south, back towards their school. They know this because the compass needle is pointing north, in the opposite direction.

*A compass needle always points north.*

Finally, Alex, Jodie, Jaan and Leah arrive at the school gates. The walk has taken just over two hours. During their walk, the children have answered all the questions they had about the village.

? If you walked all around your hometown, how many kilometres would you cover?

The children check the pedometer app on their teacher's phone. It tells them they have walked just over three kilometres. The children are surprised – they all thought they had walked further than this!

**FOCUS ON TECHNOLOGY**

Mobile phone **technology** is useful on a walk. You can download apps to show you how far you have walked and where you are on a map.

# Keeping in touch

When Alex and Leah return to their classroom, they get a map of the UK and look for their home village of Great Chesterford. Then they find the UK on a map of Europe. They can see there are lots of different countries in the continent of Europe.

The children's school is linked with two schools in Germany and Ireland. Alex, Jodie, Jaan and Leah have been learning about life in these countries.

 Is your school **twinned** with a school in another country?

They are friends with some children at a pre-school in Germany. This school is called the 'Billy Kindergarten.' In Germany, children go to Kindergarten until they are six years old, and start primary school at seven.

*The children at Billy Kindergarten sent a photo to their English friends.*

Alex, Jodie, Jaan and Leah have worked on projects with their German friends. They have designed posters and entered competitions together. The children at both schools like to keep in touch. Sometimes they make **online video calls** to say hello and swap news.

**FOCUS ON TECHNOLOGY**
Online video calls, social network sites, emails and texts are all ways of keeping in contact with people who live a long way away.

*The children like to talk to their friends in Germany online.*

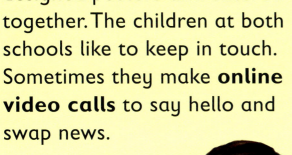

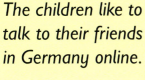

# Find the route

Can you follow the whole route on the map?

Can you locate on the map each of the places in the photos?

1

2

3

4

5

# Glossary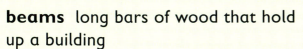

**beams** long bars of wood that hold up a building

**century** period of a hundred years

**churchyard** ground around a church, usually with graves in it

**compass** instrument that shows where north is

**county** one of the areas a country is split up into

**crop** plants that are grown to be harvested and sold

**crossroads** a point where two or more roads cross

**doctors' surgery** place where doctors see and treat patients

**GPS** network of satellites that tells you where you are on Earth

**large scale map** map which shows a lot of detail of a small area

**local business** firm that makes things or provides a service to the surrounding area

**online video call** phone call made online with a webcam, so you can see who you are talking to

**pargeting** decorative plaster patterns on the outside walls of houses

**pedestrian** someone who is walking

**pedometer app** a software download that measures how far you walk or run

**public pay phone** telephone that anyone can pay to use

**route** way you go to get to a place

**smartphone** mobile phone with computer power and connected to the Internet

**sports ground** place where people play sport

**steam train** train that burns coal to drive a steam engine

**storehouse** big building where things are kept

**technology** machinery and electronic devices developed from scientific knowledge

**thatched roof** roof made with straw, grass and reeds

**thatcher** person who builds a thatched roof

**Tudor** from 1485–1603, when England was ruled by the Tudor royal family

**twinned** towns that are twinned exchange visits and organise events together

**UK** the United Kingdom, which is the countries of England, Wales, Scotland and Northern Ireland

**unpolluted** clean and healthy

**vehicle** means of transport

**Victorian** from 1837–1901, when Victoria was Queen of Great Britain and Ireland

# Index